Stop Smile Breathe Be

~ A Guide for Awakening to Your True-OneSelf ~
The 1 Minute Mindfulness Meditation to Break Free of
Stress, Fear, or Sadness to Experience Inner-Peace and
Happiness

By: Brian Marc Zimberg

www.BrianMarc.com

Published by EHD Media
Post Office Box 192251
Miami Beach, FL 33119

Editorial: Jonathan Flexman

Table of Contents

Realizing The Lasting Inner-Peace Of Meditation Is Possible

What would life be like if no matter what happened you were able to access a deep sense of inner-peace and joy? Even if the worst things were occurring, you would know an unshakable freedom and clarity. You would be finally free of stress, anxiety, fear, sadness, depression, self-doubt and loathing. Imagine being able to connect to the most profound stillness and happiness that the greatest sages and Zen masters of all time have spoken of - all in under two minutes! This is all possible for you, and in this book I will introduce you to one of the ways in which you can immediately access this profound peace that, in *Access Points*, I call your True-OneSelf. More than that, I offer you an invitation to join a movement of awakening that is sweeping the planet. Never before have so many people been able to wake up to their True-OneSelf: the source of true creativity and joy. *Stop Smile Breathe Be* is part of a new spiritual paradigm that allows you to connect with the Divine inner-peace of meditation faster and easier than ever.

Although there are many powerful traditional practices for connecting with your True-OneSelf, none of these traditions were created for people living in the modern world. Yet our modern world is completely unprecedented. Never before have people lived with such a fast pace and so much information overload! In fact, the average modern person processes 34 gigabytes of information a day, which is more information than a person living a 100 years ago processed in an entire lifetime! So while those old, traditional practices of sitting cross-legged in a cave for 50 years in meditation may work, they aren't the most effective practices for people living in the modern world. **There is a better way**.

That is why I have created *Access Points -The Modern Life Meditation Plan* - a *modern* approach to realizing inner-peace and spiritual awakening. This plan allows you to experience all the benefits of meditation without having to go anywhere or practice meditation for long periods of time. In fact, with *Access Points* you can experience greater freedom and happiness in just a few minutes. *Access Points* can be done anywhere, anytime, without anyone even knowing you're doing it. Remarkably, the more you fully show up in your busy life, the more opportunities you have to discover greater peace, clarity, freedom and happiness.

In the modern world, we have the expertise to be able to quickly train people to grow and achieve so many things. If you want to fuel your body for peak athletic performance, then you need a nutrition plan and a fitness plan. If you want to save money and invest, you need a financial plan. The same is true for meditation and awakening to your True-OneSelf: If you want to experience real inner-peace and all the benefits of mediation, then you need a meditation plan. There is no need to rely on practices that weren't crafted specifically for modern day people because I have developed a systematic plan for awakening to the peace of mediation in every moment. It's specifically for people like you.

Access Points and SSBB are profoundly beneficial for everyone. If you are an experienced meditator, then you will be amazed at how quickly you can deepen your connection and experience of stillness. If you are seeking spiritual enlightenment, then *Access Points* will deepen your clarity and insight so you can live an Awake Life. It even makes meditation available to those who have never meditated before. So if you have heard about the benefits of meditation and always wanted to experience it, then *Access Points* is for you. It will give you the most effective way to get all the benefits of meditation, including: increased creativity, better relationships, a greater sense of purpose, and unshakable happiness and peace.

I wanted to create a system that guarantees results; a plan that systematically helps you to shift your attention away from ever-changing thoughts to the peaceful center of your True-OneSelf. In this book, you will learn core processes from *Access Points - The Modern Life Meditation Plan,* and I will share with you the #1 Access Point, called *Stop Smile Breathe Be,* or SSBB for short. You will learn about the operating systems of the mind, how they keep you stuck in the same repetitive patterns of suffering, and how to break free. I will take you through the "Past to Now Moment" exercise, where you will realize the infinity of being. You'll have the ability to completely step out of the information stream, shift your attention "out of your mind", and access the peace of Oneness, or *true* meditation, at any moment and in any place.

Imagine, if your boss is angry, you can be at peace. When your kids are crying, you can experience stillness within, and thus be more capable of helping them discover peace for themselves. In teaching the approach of *Access Points* and *Stop Smile Breathe Be,* people report that they are able to experience calm, clarity, and happiness at any time. Whether standing in line at the grocery store or stuck in traffic on the freeway, they have found, as will you, that it is possible to finally be free of the worrying mind, the doubting mind, the fearful mind, the figuring-it-out mind. You can be free of the near constant barrage of thoughts, negative emotions, and stress. Finally, you will know the true and lasting peace of real meditation.

When you connect to this true meditative happiness and peace day-to-day, it soon becomes your experience moment-to-moment. Imagine feeling freedom, joy for life and self-love, all without having to do anything. No long hours with eyes closed, no stiff legs, no mantras, nothing difficult at all. You can experience this peace in your relationships, in your work, and with yourself. You will begin to notice that your relationships become more joyful. You will find that life begins to have greater meaning. Your life becomes so abundant and joyful that you naturally contribute to those around you in meaningful ways. In your daily life, you will discover that you feel connected to spirit and Oneness, and the old stresses simply melt away.

If you're like me, or like many of the people who have personally benefited from *Access Points - the Modern Life Meditation Plan*, then I know that you have tried many things to improve your life. You have learned a lot. You have talents and wisdom. You may practice yoga to experience greater emotional balance and inner-peace. You have probably read book after book on spirituality and self-help. Maybe you have attended workshops or retreats. You may have meditated, or at least *believe* that you could benefit from meditation. Surely you've gained insights and had realizations of Oneness and greater peace, yet overtime, this peace and connection fade away. You haven't gotten the total realization of peace that you're seeking.

With *Access Points -The Modern Life Meditation Plan* you will discover what none of the other things have given you: an effective, quick, fun and profound way to experience

lasting peace at any time. What you'll find is that as you do *Stop Smile Breathe Be*, everything will start to fall into place. All the books, studies, workshops, and everything else you've done will start to really make sense. All your wisdom and talents will become more alive and vibrant. All the reading you have done on self-improvement and spirituality, all the realizations and all you've learned now "click." You will live your life effortlessly able to realize the "Now" and Oneness.

I know, without question, that it is possible for you to connect to your True-OneSelf, to soak in the beauty, peace and power of it. Finally, you can know what it is to be free of what Buddha called "suffering". You can be free of the "monkey mind". Imagine what it will be like when in any moment you are able to drop stress, worry, fear, and doubt. You can step into your soul, into the one soul of life, and have that great clarity and profound, deep inner-peace. It's here for you. It is time for this connection to stick. I can't wait for you to experience this, and for you to be able to discover the joy that arises as you apply *Access Points* and SSBB more and more in your life.

How Access Points Has Benefitted My Life And Others

For me, the results and the benefits of utilizing these techniques and these *Access Points* are profound. As you read my results and the case studies of others, ask yourself what effect these results will have in your own life.

I discovered the teaching that I share with you in this book through my own journey of awakening. In living this teaching every day of my life, I can tell you that living with access to my True-OneSelf is a life of true beauty. I live with a moment-to-moment awareness of freedom and a constant deep sense of fulfillment in a reality where everything flows. Here are some of the results I have received.

One of the biggest results I've received in living from my True-OneSelf is I am truly okay *being* myself. Regardless of what my mind says about myself, doubts I could have, self-judgements, and neuroses, there is space for all aspects of myself and I embrace all that I am. I live in the freedom of true self-expression. True self-confidence comes from this full embrace of all I am. I can tell you this is real self-power, not puffed up ego-power. Free of the common concern of what other people think, I *live* self-acceptance. I feel a constant self-love emanating from within. Since I no longer identify with my mind or personality, I am glad to welcome it all.

There is a moment-to-moment sense of freedom, like this unshakable peace, which allows all emotions to eventually dissolve. In life, I can get bothered by something. I'm a human being. I still have emotions and reactions, but none of them stick. You won't see me hours later bothered by something that happened two hours earlier. You won't see me angry or sad the next day about something that happened before. The reason that none of these things stick is because I've learned, with these Access Points, how to shift to my True-OneSelf, and this centered peace that I *really* am always takes over. This unshakable stillness dissolves those negative things. There's no reason to hold onto them because they come and go. They're not perpetuated. From that space, clarity takes over in my life.

Here is an extreme example of this unshakable peace. Years into travelling as an enlightenment teacher, I had a major depression come over me. It was the first depression of my life; a life shattering experience where I lost my job, my relationship, and my home. I even stopped teaching awakening to others (which was my true passion). I had always been an upbeat, high-energy person. It was shocking to know this level of sadness, and it gave me a compassion for others who experience this feeling more often. I was shut down...REALLY depressed. I would go to sleep crying and wake up crying. There was this jarring separation from Oneness for the first time in 10 years. I suffered and processed through the sadness and feelings of loss for a month and a half.

What brought me back to clarity, peace, and freedom from that depression? Meditation. Even though I felt disconnected for the first time in many years, sitting in meditation and connecting to my True-OneSelf gave me the capacity and the ability to truly meet the emotion of sadness, no longer making a story of it or running from it. **This**

ability to not overindulge an emotion, but meet it directly, dissolves that emotion and reveals something deeper: Oneness. This is your True-OneSelf: free of the mind, of emotion and circumstances. From that stillness, I was able to move forward in clarity, move to a new city, and start a new life which led to a new relationship and the birth of my beautiful daughter.

Life can have extreme highs and lows. Another great result of living from True-OneSelf is having the ability to handle challenges that arise in life in a whole different way. For example, I was able to go through a divorce only a few months after my daughter was born. I'm sure many of you have been in a breakup, and you know that painful time. It's like a dream dying, that feeling of a terrible loss. After a divorce, very few people accomplish friendship with their ex because of jealousy, fear, or lack of forgiveness. I am still good friends with my ex-wife. It allows us to put those things aside and recognize what's important, which is the love of our daughter. It allows her to not to be inflicted upon by jealousy, hatred and ugliness that so many couples hold for one another after divorce.

Another beautiful result from utilizing these Access Points is my relationship with my wife. I've never been with such an amazing woman and been encompassed by such a pure and unconditional love. There is an ability to be truthful, honest, and open with each other. There is space for all of it. No matter what friction may show up in our emotions or personalities, there is true acceptance and love. We are there for each other no matter what. (I love you, Barbara. Thank you!)

Acceptance of others is a result of the profound self-acceptance and self-love I spoke of above. What's great about self-acceptance is it allows you to accept other circumstances and situations "as they are", not as our thoughts say "it should be". This allows you to forgive others, to forgive the past, and to forgive yourself. When you do that, there's a greater clarity. In that clarity, of course, is love. *Access Points* has love be the focal point in your life, instead of unworthiness, anger and fear. I have deeper, more meaningful connections with the people in my life. By relating from this place of Oneness, I am blessed to have absolutely amazing relationships with my wife, my daughters, my family, my friends!

SSBB & *Access Points* offer you an unshakable ground of knowing you're fulfilled and at peace, like a continuous respite. You are okay. You are strength itself. You can handle the challenges and the things that come in life in a whole different way where you don't run from things. You are able to be present with them. This is your True-OneSelf.

What would it be like to relate to the people in your life from a perspective centered in love?

Living from True-OneSelf, I have a clear sense of purpose, meaning, and direction in my life. I don't have to try to "figure out" my purpose. Instead, my purpose arises naturally out of the core of my being. It is absolutely amazing to live life on purpose, through self-love, free from fear and shame.

This leads to one of the greatest gifts I've received from utilizing this system: I am able to share this profound teaching and experience with other people, including you! This is a gift that keeps on giving. Sharing from my own direct experience of peace is a beautiful and joyous experience. It is what I was born to do. The sharing and confidence come directly from the inner peace and stillness of True-OneSelf.

I have been blessed to share this teaching with thousands of people and witness their awakening. So many of them have had phenomenal results. I'd like to tell you a little about two of my students who had a profound transformation in their lives. They were both facing life-threatening illness, yet, by applying *Access Points* like SSBB in their lives, they were able to know peace and clarity through every challenge.

First, I'd like to tell you about Bill. I met Bill during a public meeting I held to introduce this teaching to others. Bill had been depressed for 30 years and suffered from post traumatic stress from Vietnam. He had been seeking spiritual enlightenment without success for many years. Although he had several peak experiences of happiness and bliss, they faded away, leaving him seeking for more.

This teaching resonated with Bill, and soon we began working together through a private session. I taught him some of the very same teachings I offer you in this book. After only a month, Bill began to experience profound transformations that remained with him for the rest of his life.

As a result of his awakening to his True-OneSelf, Bill reconnected with his daughter, from whom he had been estranged for years. They were able to share the love and closeness that they had been missing for so long.

Bill had long denied himself the pleasures of life that he desired. By freeing himself from his mind and depression, he let go of much of the emotional baggage that he had carried for years. He was able to allow himself to accept abundance and discover the joy of giving *and receiving*. As a result, he received a rare financial VA compensation that allowed him to buy the dream car he had long wanted.

Bill had a lifelong dream of living in Hawaii that he had never realized. Shortly after awakening to his True-OneSelf, he fulfilled this dream by moving there. Once he arrived in Hawaii, he achieved the goal of owning his own condo across from the ocean in Waikiki. He quickly met wonderful friends and forged meaningful, fulfilling relationships. They explored the islands and all the adventures offered in this paradise. He refound his joy of playing guitar, and he shared the gift of music at the beach and in local bars. All of this came as a result of his realization of a deeper fulfillment and happiness.

When Bill discovered that he had terminal cancer, he met it with deep peace. What a blessing that his daughter was able to come to Hawaii and live with him. As he entered Hospice and grew closer to death, he lived each day with an abiding clarity and love. With his daughter and friends by his side, being his True-OneSelf was a source of inspiration for those around him. He had touched on all of their lives.

"My only job is to witness this perfect moment unfolding." - *Bill*

Next, I'd like to tell you about Marsha. When we met, she was living a life that seemed "pretty good" by most standards, but she couldn't shake the sense that something was wrong. She was constantly stressed by trying to balance marriage, a child, and a full-time career. Living a life that was always GO GO GO and DO DO DO, she was increasingly anxious and had begun a downward spiral of self-sabotage and excessive drinking. She was so addicted to the compulsion of always **doing** something, that she couldn't be fully present in her own life.

I began teaching Marsha *Access Points*, including *Stop Smile Breathe Be*, and her life started to turn around quickly. In fact, she reported experiencing a greater sense of peace and spaciousness in her moment-to-moment life after only a short time. She stopped drinking without even trying. As a result of connecting with her True-OneSelf, she grew more loving and closer to her husband, and was able to really be present and appreciate her child more than ever. She discovered this unshakable happiness and peace at her core and experienced a new approach to living in balance.

Not long after Marsha learned *Access Points*, she discovered that she had breast cancer. Previously, such a revelation would have left her in a frantic state. I'm sure you'd agree, finding out that you have cancer has to be one of life's scariest experiences. Imagine taking tests and waiting to see if you're going to live or you're going to die. Has this cancer spread or not? When she was informed by the doctor that her only chance was to undergo chemotherapy and surgery, she was able to meet that crisis with calm and clarity. Do you listen to your doctor, or do you go for a second opinion? Her intuition flew in the face of the doctor's recommendation. Learning to *access* peace and clarity at a moment's notice undoubtedly gave Marsha the courage to do what was right for her. As the result of listening to her intuition, she is healthy and happy. In fact, she says that facing this challenge as her True-OneSelf gave her an appreciation for the cancer. She knew it was a gift to be called to face it and deal with with her shadow, pain, fear, and sadness. Connecting to

Oneness, she continues to experience daily that same courage, strength, and peace at her core.

Both of these examples are circumstances that could happen to any of us. Imagine the worst thing that could happen to you, as it did for Marsha. How would that be for you? What would that look like for you? Look back in the last few years of your life. Remember something really painful, maybe something really sad, really difficult, or some challenge you had to face. Imagine being able to meet that challenge with complete peace and clarity, as well as to face other hardships of life with a centered calmness. Imagine being able to shift out of fear, out of anger, out of sadness and connect to your True-OneSelf at any moment. From that, such a beautiful thing will happen in your life. You will be able to have a greater sense of self-love, self-certainty, and self-esteem. You become more present in life, much like Bill. You will naturally attract abundance and true friendships. You can attract the things you've always wanted. Not because you had worked so hard to get them, but because you are ever deeper into awakening to Oneness. Releasing deeper and deeper into self-realization and inner-peace. Into being okay with yourself and who you are. Discovering your True-OneSelf. All of this is possible through *Access Points* and *Stop Smile Breathe Be.*

Common Obstacles To Meditation And Awakening

As you begin to practice *Access Points* & *SSBB* in this book, you will soon discover the same peace and happiness that mystics and sages have pointed to for centuries. But if it really is that simple, why aren't more people experiencing this state of true meditation more often? The problem is there appears to be many obstacles to realizing this meditative peace and connection to Oneness. In my experience, here are some of the most common problems I have heard:

"Meditation takes too much time. I just don't have the extra hour a day to meditate."
By far, the most common obstacle to self-realization is the belief that it requires hours of grueling meditation practice every day. The majority of modern people simply don't have that much time in a day, and so we don't dedicate ourselves to practicing meditation. People are also unable to commit to a program they feel takes a longer period of time.

"I can't sit still for that long. My legs and back bother me too much, and I get too distracted."
Another common belief is that meditation requires a certain posture in order to do it correctly. Most of us have the image in our mind of the cross-legged yogi or monk. But when we try to do that, we become uncomfortable. Often times our legs fall asleep. We become restless. For most of us this can become an obstacle to connecting to the meditative state. Even if you *can* sit for a long time, nothing seems to happen.

"My mind is too active. I just can't stop the racing thoughts."
We often hear the message that enlightenment, or self-realization, is the cessation of all thought. We're taught that the goal of meditation is to stop thought. But our minds are active and loud. We cannot seem to stop our thoughts. The mental chatter is loud and distracting. And so our active minds become yet another obstacle.

"I have tried lots of different systems and techniques, but none of them really worked for me."
Disillusionment can also be an obstacle to the meditative state of self-realization and inner-peace because after many years of applying various books and spiritual practices without lasting results, some people give up entirely. People in this situation often simply don't want to sign up for yet another program that over-promises and under-delivers in their daily lives.

"I can't meditate because it conflicts with my religion."
Because these people associate meditation with Eastern religions, they are afraid to take up a practice of their own. Because they don't want to do something that will be problematic in their own religious life, they miss out on the benefits of connecting with their True-OneSelf.

"The feeling is hard to reach, and even harder to keep."
Bliss is another huge obstacle to awakening to your True-OneSelf. So many people believe that awakening means reaching some special state or blissful feeling all the time. Maybe they once had that experience and they are struggling to get it back or maintain it. Fundamentally, we may know about "presence" or "being in the now", and want to be in Oneness all the time. Yet, we are stuck identified with our minds.

"Meditation sounds nice, but I need help now, not after 50 years of practice. Meditation is something I will look into once I've sorted out my personal and emotional life."

The common misconception is that meditation is a practice that one must engage in for many years in order to begin to reap the benefits. So many people put off meditation because they want short-term benefits that they believe they can only find elsewhere.

"Everytime I think I have it figured out...it doesn't work. Maybe I need help."

The solo journey without expert guidance can get convoluted and circular. Having a mentor or a guide is essential for most people in order to awaken to their True-OneSelf. Think about this. You can hike up a treacherous mountain on your own, yet a guide that has been to the top many times will certainly speed up your efforts while helping you avert pitfalls and diversions along the way.

Testimonials

Clearly there are many obstacles to a successful mediation practice and awakening to your True-OneSelf. The process of *Access Points - The Modern Life Meditation Plan*, including SSBB which I teach you in this book, solves all of these problems. In spite of all these obstacles, the clients below were successful at breaking through and having major life transformations. You can have these results too!

Brian Marc was able to point out and invite me to face a state of being within me, a silence, and an endless place of peace that is always there no matter what may be occurring around me. As I continue to shift my attention to this internal place throughout my daily life, I become more impactful in shaping a positive environment for myself and those around me. Brian has showed me to live from that place, my true-self. I am free because I am now a witness to my actions and experiences! He will really get you out of your mind and plugged into a realm of endless possibility!
- Dwyn Aldryn - Celebrity Fitness Trainer

Before *SSBB* & *The Modern Life Meditation Plan*, I had a very difficult time making my mind still. Meditation was really annoying and time consuming. Yet, I knew it was crucial for my well-being. I needed to find a solution, and this worked better than I could have ever imagined! I still find it amazing that it can be this simple. I can suffer in my mind and emotions, or I can be free as my True-OneSelf. It is a choice. I never could have believed it is this easy to stay in the moment, every moment. It is fresh and profound every time.

- Gwen T. - Portland, Oregon

I now have the greatest clarity of my True-OneSelf, always present, here and now. It is a whole new life. Brian's *Access Points* have a simplicity and beauty. They cut through so many ideas and misconceptions. I was able to connect to the space of love and freedom that I had only experienced a few times in all my "spiritual work". This process works and really frees you from identification with the mind, revealing peace around every corner. Daily, I go deeper into the core of truth and love, and I know I am impacting the world as we move closer to this realization for all humanity. Get this course and just do it!

- Marianne L. - Chicago, Illinois

Access Points trained me to no longer believe the self-destructive thoughts and habits that have been haunting me for years. When the dark feelings creep in, I am able to be present and it transforms to serenity and joy. This is really moment-to-moment. It is not just a peak high, like so many things I've tried in my life that didn't last. I really am not my thoughts or my emotions. If you want the peace that meditation promises and to be free of depression, I've never seen a technique as simple and effective as *Stop Smile Breathe Be*.

- Manuela M. - Rio de Janeiro, Brazil

Thank you so much for your help, Brian.

Keeping my attention on the sense that "I AM" feels so good. Thoughts don't disturb me as before. I feel like I am free and expanding. Today, when I was in the city, I noticed how effortlessly it is to keep my attention on OneSelf by using the *Access Points*. It opened up a beautiful stillness. Before, I would get so caught up in thought activity. In the city, there is so much noise! People are running here and there with a lot of stress. It is beautiful to just BE, and to not be disturbed by all. It is only a little shift in attention from being aware of things, thoughts, and stories to being aware of Oneness. Thank you again!

- Julie H. - NYC, New York

Dear Brian,

Being at the seminar was wonderful. Since being with you, I have let go of beating "myself" up because I did not give enough energy to being aware all day long. I realize that I am Here always, living from the present moment. Looking back at the past and wishing it was different is rather a ridiculous habit and waste of energy...especially if you take it seriously, which I did. What a tremendous relief...just accepting "what is" with a gentleness that wasn't there before. No more looking for this moment to be different than it is. Funny, one can be so blind to what is so perfectly obvious. Thank you for sharing your beauty, clarity and presence.

- Cee - Greenville, North Carolina

I was in a psych ward with suicidal depression. My doctors were considering electro-shock therapy. (I didn't even know they still did that!) A year later, I was a bit better and trying to put my life back together. I came home to find my wife had packed it in and left me a note on the table. This was one month shy of our 20th Wedding Anniversary. So I had another round or two of suicidal depression.

Two years later, I started attending meetings with Brian. I had been chasing Enlightenment for more than 30 years, but Brian wasn't saying the things that I had come to expect. I requested a private session. We met on the cliffs overlooking the beach at Santa Monica. With just a bit of defiance in my voice, I explained to Brian that...while I was definitely ready for something...I wasn't at all sure whether he had anything I was looking for. So we talked a bit, and he guided me in meditation. I suddenly realized that the smallest, little, subtle shift had taken place, and my life was transformed. I grinned like an idiot, and Brian's eyes twinkled a bit.

My State of Being has not faltered in the slightest since that moment on the cliffs. I live every moment in The Present. I had empty parts inside of me, but now I am whole...complete. The Present Moment is the primary focus of my life. My "life situation" or "my drama" is a distant second. All of that drama is pretty inconsequential. It means so little.

The truth is, if for some very bizarre reason I needed to leave the Present Moment, I wouldn't have the slightest idea how to go about it. In a sense, I AM The Present Moment. My life and The Present Moment just continue to be more and more intertwined. It's more and more difficult to separate the two. I am the awareness. *I AM*. Thank you, Brian.

- Bill - Van Nuys, California

How I Lost My Mind To Get Out Of My Mind - My Journey Of Awakening

Throughout my childhood, my parents were deeply into self-help and personal development teachings. I was raised around it. And so it was, when I was 18, I attended my first Anthony Robbins weekend event with my family. This event changed my life, but probably not in the way that the organizers would have intended! Along with the hundreds of other attendees, I walked over a bed of hot coals the first night of the weekend. This feat is intended to shake the attendees out of their limited belief systems and wake them up to their greater potential. For me, it literally knocked me right "out of my mind". Walking over the hot coals the first time, I was exhilarated. I knew that my life beforehand had been limited by fears, and now...BOOM! Anything was possible! When I walked over the bed of hot coals for the second and third time, I knew that I could accomplish anything. I felt that power coming from within me. By the time I walked over the coals for the fourth time, something broke free in my mind. It was all of the beliefs that society had placed on me, all the programming of limitation. I was free from the limited beliefs and the separate identity called "ME". Without the concept of ME, I *truly* felt connected with each and every person.

If walking over hot coals was ecstatic, what followed was hell. What I believed to be real, was real to me. What meaning I gave things, was the meaning I believed. At first this was all very beautiful, but as my thoughts got faster and faster I began building a story that wasn't true. I had broken free of the limitations of consensus reality, but I was still trapped, believing my own mind, believing my own delusions of grandeur. *Later in life, I realized we are all actually living stuck in our minds, in a delusion all of the time. Real freedom IS free from the mind's beliefs, meanings, thoughts, and perceptions.*

My parents worried about me, and they took me to psychiatrist friend who said I may be having a manic episode. He prescribed a pill and said in a few days I would come back down to Earth. But I kept running away from them daily. Literally. They were exhausted trying to find me. They kept trying to get me to "take the pill" so I would snap out of it and be ok. Things progressively got worse, and Hell took the form of a psychiatric ward when my family admitted me into a hospital.

I found myself drugged up such that I drooled, my thoughts were slow, and my speech was slurred. My muscles cramped. They kept giving me more pills. White pills and green pills. When I looked around I was in shock, and I snapped out of the delusional thinking of the week before. "What the hell am I doing here? What's happening to me?" I realized I was being doped up by the staff as my shoulders were cramping in pain. I asked for help, but no one would listen. The nurses would patronize me, but not care to help. I was truly alone here.

I wanted out of this place, and the only people I could think to turn to was my family. "They'll help me," I thought. I called my mom and dad and told them the nurses were drugging me up with all these pills. They would just tell me "take the medicine and everything will be ok." The only people I thought I could turn to couldn't help me. I was trapped. What was happening? How do I get out of here? I started to fake taking the pills. I knew if my parents saw me, they would get me out of here. So I attempted to get attention by creating a ruckus to shake things up. I started screaming. I grabbed the pool balls off the table, hitting them on the thick glass windows. I thought they would call my parents to come see me. Instead, three big men came in, grabbed me, and threw me in a small room.

I was locked in this room with metal mesh over the windows. The room was bare except for a small mattress on the floor. I was treated like a caged animal in a laboratory. I cried out for my parents. I felt trapped and truly alone. I laid on that mattress in a fetal position. It was like a hell within a hell. Alone. The patronizing voice came over the intercom and said, "If you're a good boy, we will let you out." I honestly feared that I would never be free again. Like my life was over. In tears, I prayed and called out for G-d's help.

It was there in that hell, that dark and hopeless place, that I had one of the most influential experiences of my life.I felt a powerful opening to true inner knowing. I knew love beyond anything I had known before that.

It was there in that dark and hopeless place, that I had one of the most influential experiences of my life. I discovered an inner-knowing of love and connection. Not from some voice, but instead a total clarity of being - I *knew* beyond doubt that I would be alright. That I was loved and protected. In a fetal position, I rocked back and forth on the bare mattress reassuring myself over and over again, "You're okay. You'll get out of here." Magically, my father came the next day. They had me so doped up and cramping that he couldn't believe it. He quickly hired a lawyer and got me released. In fact is, if the psychiatrist *didn't* agree to release me, I would have appeared in court doped up like that, and a judge could have sent me to the state hospital.

And so it was that I began to seek for a deeper meaning, to discover what my purpose in life was, and to know that connection to peace I discovered on the mattress in that horrible hospital room.

Shortly after I entered college, I found that I honestly couldn't relate to the interests of most of my peers. They were interested in partying and sex, but for me, those pursuits seemed pale considering that I had recently fought for my life, my freedom, and well-being.

I followed my heart, I left college, and moved to NYC to study acting with renown teachers Herbert Berghof and Uta Hagen. It was then that I started recognizing that, though I was successful at many endeavors, I still had this bad temper, fears, doubts, and insecurities inside of me. So I went about working on myself. I'm sure many of you have been there. We struggle on fixing ourselves, making ourselves better. The problem with a lot of self-help books is the idea of "working on one's self" is often rooted in the concept that "I need to be fixed," "I am broken," or "I need to be better." I read countless self-help books, lifted weights, and got really good at changing and fixing my habits. I was actually growing in a lot of ways. It was exhilarating at first, but eventually the idea that "I need to fix myself" or "be better" became my mind's new whip; beating me up where I was not better. Deep down, I knew this stood contrary to the experience I had with great certainty on that mattress in that hospital room: The knowing I am "FULLY OKAY and LOVED". So we get frustrated on the journey of self-help because we pull a weed or "fix something," and then a new weed grows right back. We still feel disconnected and a need to be "better". Shame and fear are still running the show, and after awhile...it gets exhausting.

My success at self-improvement only left a temporary feeling of accomplishment - never a lasting fulfillment. At this time, I was also experiencing the beginnings of disillusionment about success overall. I would set out to accomplish something and I would. Study acting in NYC? Yes. With world-renowned coaches? Double yes. Create a profitable business? Yes. Raise money and create a movie? Yes. Go to Hollywood and get signed by agents? Yes. So was this what life was about? Think of an idea, create it, and achieve it? Over and over again? Only later did I hear Buddha explain suffering. "We never will be fulfilled from worldly things because they leave us with only a temporary experience of happiness." I wanted the real thing. The thing that touched my soul on that hospital mattress. There is a frustration when we realize that nothing we do *really* gives us the happiness we crave. At some point we realize this, and there is a "hopelessness" that arises. Like an existential, "what's the point?"

So yes, I acted, made money with a business, and starred in a feature film I wrote and produced. It was beautiful to be creative, to collaborate and flow. Then I got to Hollywood. I said I would do all of this and I did! I had Leonardo DiCaprio's management company wining and dining me. I signed with two, Top-5 agents; one for acting and one for writing. I set out to create a dream, and I was about live it...

It was then, at 28 years old and just after the Hollywood premiere of my movie, that I had my first truly transcendental, mystical experience on psychedelic mushrooms in Joshua Tree Desert. In that clarity, I knew that G-d was Oneness and reality without question. I went home and fervently started writing about spirit and Oneness. I read a page to my mother, and she told me it sounded like Deepak Chopra. Having no idea who he was, I bought "The 7 Spiritual Laws of Success" and I was hooked. I was a bonafide spiritual seeker.

Once I had that spiritual itch, the spiritual calling which many of us have had, I read every book I could get my hands on. I started doing yoga, and diligently worked at meditating. Meditation was difficult at first. Sitting still, my knees would hurt, my neck and back bothered me. The mind chatter was loud and distracting. Following the directions of Paramahansa Yogananda, I learned to sit and focus on the third eye. As I focused, I excelled in this technique and I started to experience bliss. In this state, my highest self began to download mystical understandings. I shared these understandings with religious and spiritual teachers, and they confirmed that I was receiving true mystical knowledge.

I continued to search for that elusive "enlightenment". I participated in workshops and seminars with world-renowned spiritual and personal-development teachers. I devoured more books. I learned so much. I continued to have deeper realizations and deeper epiphanies, but ultimately nothing led to that everlasting fulfillment and spiritual realization that meditation was supposed to offer. All the highs, the bliss, and the realizations started to get in the way because my mind started to co-op all my experiences. It wasn't enough. It wasn't quite full.

I still felt trapped in my own neuroses, in my own mind...in Brian. *Maybe you've been there. The mind starts to incorporate all the things you learned and kind of uses it against you. It's like you know too much and you have too many understandings, when, in fact, the peace of meditation is beyond the mind's comprehension. And I knew that too. Sound familiar?* I'd become spiritualized. I had developed a spiritual-ego mind. I had a spiritual answer for everything. I could meditate for hours, and I would walk around with a big grin. Life was blissful, and I began teaching others to connect to this Bliss. Yet there was some deep contentment and lasting fulfillment that I couldn't reach. Meditation was supposed to offer that to me, but it was incapable of doing so.

What turned it all around was reading from the great sage Osho. He suggested I stop looking for an experience in my mediation. Stop knowing what's coming next. I've read that many times before, yet this time, I got it. I sat still and didn't care for what was coming next. I didn't try to get to a blissful sensation or feeling. The key realization was that I didn't try to achieve anything in the meditation. I didn't try to **do** anything to **get** something. In that, there was vastness, or what I've referred to as this "totality of all things". A profound stillness and an all-pervading Oneness overcame me.

Years later, I realized I wanted to talk to a living enlightenment "teacher". One who was as awake as I was, and hopefully more. One that could validate what I knew to be absolute truth and could also point out where I was off or trapped. I had seen a picture of Gangaji and heard some of her audio recordings so I looked her up when I first returned to LA, and, as it turned out, she was coming into town that week - her first time in 2 years! What a coincidence - yet, of course, we know there is no such thing.

I went to a public meeting with her, and I went up on stage. There, we looked at one another, eye to eye. I saw OneSelf everywhere, yet this time it was OneSelf looking back at me. MySelf looking at my MySelf, and I thought, "This woman knows as much as I do, or more. She sees the truth of OneSelf." It was a true meeting - Self meeting Self.

What turned things around even more was this realization that I needed to surrender all ideas of myself. I needed to stop seeking for more and drop everything. Then, BOOM...in dropping everything I started to see, with Gangaji's guidance and the power of Ramana Maharshi's Self Inquiry, this vast array of techniques and methods that I use to stay identified with my mind and separate.

It was about 6 months later in the shower that I realized I could LITERALLY stop believing all my thoughts. At times I had understood this, but only partially. Yet, in that moment, I saw deeper than ever before: OneSelf is *always* here, free from all thoughts...and even when thoughts are here! When I got that, I laughed out loud so hard. In gratitude, I enjoyed the beauty of life as the water flowed over my head - pure Oneness.

I started to experience the joy and the peace of my True-OneSelf moment-to-moment. I *AM* my True-OneSelf right here, right now. Oneness was no longer an idea, thought, or feeling I wanted. It was a constant reality. Freedom and peace. Meditation came to be something that wasn't just when I was sitting trying to *do* meditation. Meditation was now moment-to-moment.

It all came from my learning to not believe my mind. *Can you imagine what it would be like to not believe your mind?*

Being released from the burden of believing the "monkey mind"? That is glorious. It's like being freed from a trap that you might not even realize you're in.

With blessings from Gangaji, I was invited to start sharing as an enlightenment teacher. I guided seekers (as "Brian Qara") in the spirit of this invitation to awaken. People came from all over the world, and I was able to help them shift "out of their minds" - the key to real meditation and awakening.

What I've realized is that everybody was still trying so hard to get to what is already right here. What's in the way? They are stuck in their minds, separate, and lack the access to shift out of their thoughts and identity to, what I like to call, your True-OneSelf. The ground of all being. Oneness.

They had yoga or meditation techniques, past teachers, and books. They had these different practices or paths that were going to give them fulfillment, but they didn't work. These techniques didn't match up to our modern way of life.-The static of our modern day, with the noise and the loudness of all those 43 gigabytes of information, compounds everything upon us.-I needed to distill for people a way to directly cut through all that noise. All those patterns and trances of the mind that keep us stuck inside of our heads don't allow us to experience Oneness right NOW. This is where the meditation experience *actually* happens.

I travelled the US sharing this for five years. I was blessed to help guide and witness the awakening of 1000's of people. Yet, I realized that something unique and new had to express itself through me. It was at that time that my life turned upside down, and I faced my darkest shadows. I was ripped away from my past and everything I knew.

This was the depression I described earlier. It was anything but pleasant. It was a total upheaval. I lost my girlfriend, and I moved across the country. I formally stopped teaching. Once I broke free of the depression, through meditation, I connected deeper with OneSelf. In contrast, this time I was grounded in a new way and became a father. After this period of reconfiguration, my most powerful and direct teaching to date began to take shape. I began to offer this teaching informally to friends and students, and I discovered that I was able to help people wake up more quickly and simply than ever before.

When I found this solution, I dug deep. I started analyzing, looking at every single pattern of the mind - what I later called in *Access Points*, "The Survival Animal". I started studying the Enneagram, Spiral Dynamics, and looking at different patterns and ways that we can keep ourselves trapped with different trances in our mind. The more survival patterns that were exposed, the deeper the realization of OneSelf.

I wanted to see how it was it that these students who came to me kept falling back into the traps of the mind. I discovered and developed key tools that can be done skillfully and quickly at a moment's notice. I was a single father working a regular job, and even though I was not sharing publicly, people continued to seek me out for this new process of meditation and awakening. As they learned to step out of their mind, they too started to experience meditation throughout the day. They experienced the True-OneSelf that *is* meditation - that *is* enlightenment. I distilled these discoveries down to the most effective tools and processes possible. I called them *Access Points - The Modern-Life Meditation Plan*, a modern approach to experiencing all the benefits of meditation and awakening.

The Myths

I struggled for many years trying to overcome the obstacles of realizing true meditation. Eventually, I succeeded in knowing stillness and unshakable peace. And when I did that, I finally discovered the secret to experiencing true meditation moment-to-moment. Do you want to know what I realized? There are so many myths about meditation, what enlightenment is, and how to achieve it, and it is really only these myths that stand in the way! So we need to throw out these myths. Once and for all, I'm going to shatter some of the most common misconceptions about meditation and awakening which hold people back from discovering their True-OneSelf and the peace within.

Stop Your Thoughts

The aim of meditation and the path to awakening is stopping all thought, right? This is yet another one of the most common misunderstandings that so many people believe. They work so hard trying to stop their minds because they think that is the goal of meditation. But let me explain something to you, which might sound silly, but it's true. The only thing that's trying to make the mind be quiet *IS* the mind! This is important to hear. So think about this. (Pun intended.) I've sat down with people who think they've learned to meditate, done yoga, or meditated for years. I can see the strain they exert in trying to stop thoughts. They'll focus really hard. Of course, the harder they focus on the thoughts, the more difficult it becomes. Eventually, they have to give up because it's just impossible to stop thoughts by following other thoughts about stopping thoughts.

So hear this: YOU DON'T NEED TO STOP YOUR THOUGHTS. I promise you this! It doesn't matter how loud or quiet, how tranquil or racing your mind is. The peace and stillness of meditation is happening even when you are thinking! It is possible to allow all thoughts to come and go. Allow your thoughts to just be as they are, like a radio playing in the background. Like a distant conversation happening "over there", away from here. When the root of your attention rests with the core of "being", the essence of meditation, the stillness of meditation, can exist even when your mind is loud. To be able to connect to that stillness, whether your mind is talking and loud, or whether your mind is quiet, is *true* meditation. The key to experiencing meditation, as you will learn in the next chapter, is shifting your attention from mind to your True-OneSelf.

I Have To Sit Still

One of the myths about meditation that so many people believe is the notion that you have to sit still, motionless, in some cross-legged posture. It's easy to see why people believe this, too. After all, there are many teachings, traditions, and practices that say exactly that. What I can assure you of, what I know with absolute certainty, is the idea that meditation requires physical restraint is not true! True meditation and the meditative state is happening whether you are sitting or walking. It is occurring regardless of movement or non-movement. The stillness of meditation occurs moment-to-moment, all the time. True meditation is not dependent on certain physical conditions because it is already present regardless of any conditions. What meditation *really* is: learning to shift your attention out of your mind to the stillness that is already present. It is true that aligning our bodies and resting can have lots of benefits, but having to sit still is in no way a requirement for being aware of the stillness that resides within. I meet so many people who are so hard on them themselves because they're trying to sit still and not move. That becomes what their meditation practice is about. The irony is that fixation on the perfect meditative posture is, itself, an obstacle to experiencing the meditation that is already present. Although sitting still in meditation can be quite effective, the truth is that whether you sit still, scratch your nose, walk, or jump up and down, it is possible to shift your attention out of your mind and recognize true meditation here and now.

It's Against My Religion

Another myth about meditation is that you can't do it because it's in contradiction to your religion. Often, meditation is thought of as an Eastern practice. And yet the truth is that there are actually different types of contemplation meditation in *ALL* religions. Again, we teach in *Access Points* that the key of meditation is to actually shift your attention out of your mind. In many religions it's used as a form of devotion, clarity, and getting a clear alignment with the Creator. Meditation actually does *NOT* stand in the way of your religious beliefs or your ability to follow through with your religion. On the contrary, it actually helps you be even more devoted in your religion...if that's your true calling. It gives you the space and clarity for greater connection - a fuller devotion is possible. Even more so, *Stop Smile Breathe Be* and *Access Points - The Modern Meditation Plan* are done in a modern way in an ordinary day. You don't need certain crystals around you, you don't need to hear certain sounds, you don't need to sit down in front of a statue.

Find Your Bliss

A huge myth about meditation and awakening is the belief that the goal is to have a "blissful feeling" or high. It is true that often in a moment of deep realization or meditation we may experience bliss - a feeling of deep peace in the body - and that experience is beautiful. In it, we get a clear taste Oneness - a communion with all that is. Yet I have to tell you straight out, if you are doing meditation to get to that blissful feeling, then you are actually *adding* to your struggle and suffering. You're missing out on what is even deeper than the bliss! Deeper than bliss? Yes. You see experiences are temporary. They come and go. The peace that real meditation brings is a peace that does *not* come and go. It is a constant inner peace. It's a connection to your True-OneSelf that is permanent and always here. It is more solid than temporary bliss, and it is ultimately more rewarding. It offers you a deep ground of being that is your true nature. What do you really want? A temporary high, or a lasting, centered, ground of fulfillment that you can connect with at any moment?

There is a metaphor of a finger pointing to the moon. The experiences we have of bliss are the finger, and the deep centered inner-peace of your True-OneSelf is the moon. In truth, what you really want is the moon - and not to get stuck on the finger. So often, people sit in meditation and, instead of knowing how to shift attention to their True-OneSelf, they are "doing" meditation to "get to" bliss. This is a major trap because the mind is looking for a familiar feeling from the past that it already knows. It puts us back into a seeking mode, and it is the mind's seeking for temporary states that is the root of suffering and struggle. We may get a temporary hit or high, but after, we are again left with a void. The mind thinks the answer is to DO something to seek out another hit of bliss. So this "seeking" for bliss is another mind trap, and it never allows one to truly know real peace. It is no different than a junky looking for his next fix. It is like being a beggar, seeking over and over again for permanent fulfillment from something temporary. That, my friends, is basically Buddha's definition of suffering. Many meditation practices leave us unable to meet our real lives day-to-day with true peace. I created *Access Points* so you are able to shift to profound centered peace and not be a beggar for a "hit of bliss".

So often people on the journey to spiritual awakening think that it "looks" a certain way. Like walking around as a "blissed out" person, always smiling, with no negative emotions ever appearing, and life always being perfectly groovy. It is the mythical, ideal permanent state that inhibits our true evolution. The truth of who you are at the core is always permanently at peace and still. Yet your story will still have its ups and downs. You will still have a personality and have all sorts of emotions. The truth of awakening and living an Awake Life is actually an allowing of all circumstances, emotions - good or bad - to flow as you are present to them. You are allowed to have your experiences without avoiding them or being run by them. Your core identification shifts from the mind and limited, separate self, to your true, limitless nature. As the famous Zen line goes, "Before enlightenment chop wood, after enlightenment chop wood." This really means that everything changes, and nothing changes. Your attention is freed from the trap of a separate survival animal to the ever present glory and peace of Oneself.

It Takes Too Long

Many people also seem to hold the idea that meditation requires a lot of time. Since many people feel that they already don't have enough time in the day, this belief becomes a very real obstacle. Well, let me tell you some good news. You don't need to give an hour, 30 minutes, or even 15 minutes of your time to start experiencing true meditation. One of the greatest benefits you get when you start to implement *Stop Smile Breathe Be* on a regular basis is it only takes 1 to 3 minutes each time you do it. You can literally do it anytime and anywhere! It doesn't interrupt your life in any way, time, or place. So time is not really an issue. In fact, the whole design of *Access Points - The Modern Meditation Plan* is that they flow and work along with your daily life. You start developing a habit of shifting out of mind and into meditation throughout the day...everyday.

I invite you to let go of all these myths right now. When you let go of these myths, you are taking a huge step toward true awakening. You need to drop all you think you know about meditation and awakening. The mediation that is right for you is one that meets you now in your modern, really post-modern, life. You are letting go of your allegiance to your mind that keeps you stuck in fear and anxiety. And when you do this, you naturally begin to notice a greater peace and happiness.

As you go through this book and the *Access Points* processes, including *Stop Smile Breathe Be*, you will learn how to consciously connect with your True-OneSelf at any moment in your life. Then you'll know true meditation, which is true power and true creativity.

The Access Points Process

The Blueprint to "Get Out of Your Mind" and Shift to Your True-OneSelf

Now it's time to get into the most exciting part of this book. In the following sections I am going to take you through an exciting journey of self-discovery and give you everything you need to know to begin experiencing your True-OneSelf immediately. Here's what we'll be covering:

First, we'll talk about the amazing power of attention. You'll learn how you are already using this power all the time, and how you can begin to harness this power in order to become aware of your True-OneSelf at any moment. You can do this simply by shifting your attention "out of your mind." I'll walk you through this and give you exercises you can use to get more experience and practice.

Next, I'll share with you a deeper understanding of what your mind is and how it works. You'll start to recognize the *Main Patterns of the mind* and how it uses these to survive. Far from what most spiritual teachings may lead you to believe, your mind is certainly NOT the enemy, though it *can* delude you. You will see clearly how the patterns and programs of your mind consistently create all limitations and suffering. Your mind is designed to protect you, and that is a good thing when it comes to protecting the body. However, your mind mistakenly also wants to protect itself and maintain its identity and its specialness. This step is important because, in just being aware of the four main patterns, you will notice a release from suffering and an expansion of freedom.

Next, I'll explain how to effectively discern between what is real and what is false, so that you can use everything you've learned so far in order to begin to experience greater peace in your everyday life. You're going to learn *The Wisdom Discernment* of what comes and goes and what is always here. That which never changes is absolutely reliable, and that's what we're looking for in the meditative state. The fulfillment we're looking for is not one that changes or comes and goes, but it's the changeless space that holds all change. You're going to get to see that the unchanging ground of being, true fulfillment, is actually right here and now.

And then I will share with you the number one *Access Point* of *The Modern Life Meditation Plan*: *Stop Smile Breathe Be*, or *SSBB* for short. It is an amazingly powerful way in which you can experience your True-OneSelf and the peace of being at any time, no matter where you are, or who you're with.

I'm so excited to share all this with you. It's your birthright to know inner peace. You can do this! Follow through with these steps. Learn what there is to learn here. I'm going to guide you through it every step of the way. You will soon discover tools that connect you to the peace of meditation in any moment. It will free you of stress, fear, sadness, or anxiety. You're will be able to experience great clarity, creativity, and peace. So let's jump right in.

The Power Of Attention

Real meditation is simply being able to shift your attention *away* from your mind and *to* stillness. When we learn to take our attention off of our mind, we see what real stillness is. Stillness is another word for inner peace, awareness, being or presence. This is immediate. It doesn't require long hours sitting in a particular posture while reciting a mantra. It can happen in a moment. This moving of attention to stillness is what I call "getting out of your mind."

Getting out of your mind is the essence of true meditation, and it is very easy to do using the power of your attention. What I want to show you is that the core of your attention is stuck in your mind. Your attention is with your story. Caught in thoughts and emotions, the mental noise. To experience true meditation you need to move your attention off of that. You will naturally discover your True-OneSelf when your attention shifts out of your mind to awareness itself.

In order to shift your attention out of your mind, you first need to know how to move your attention. The easiest way to understand this is to experience it for yourself, which you can do in an instant. I'm going to share with you a simple exercise that you can do to get a taste of this.

Exercise: Moving Attention

The first thing you need to realize and see is that YOU have the power of attention. The power of attention means that you have the ability to move your attention. You do this all the time without even realizing it. It is so simple and obvious that you have overlooked it. For a moment, what I'd like you to do is to move your attention to your shirt (assuming that you wearing one. Otherwise, select something else.) Just take a moment and look at your shirt and see what color it is. Ok? That was pretty simple, right? It is that simple to move your attention. You saw what color your shirt is. You moved your eyes. You looked. And your attention moved to the shirt.

Let's do it again for a moment. I know this might seem kind of silly, but you're going to get the point very clearly if you're able to follow this. So play along for real. This time, look down to the floor and see what color the floor is. Hopefully now you can see that you can move your attention very easily. So you have this power to move your attention, but normally your attention is stuck in your mind.

Let me give you an example. When you're driving a car, the core of your attention is on staying in the lines, your speed limit, driving, and operating the car safely. At least, I hope that's the case! Of course, you can turn the radio on and off, or you can be on the phone talking to somebody. You can be doing all these things with your peripheral attention, yet still your core attention is focused on driving the car, where you're headed, and where you're going.

So really get this...*Your suffering arises from the fact that the core of your attention is habitually in your mind.* That means that most of the time your main focus is in your mind, paying attention to its commentary. But just imagine what happens when the core of your attention actually shifts to being *outside* of your mind! *This is the crucial first step for true meditation.*

If you'd like to go deeper and have me personally guide you through this exercise and the Access Points Processes, register now for *SSBB - Awakening to Your True-OneSelf* - a FREE Live Global online seminar at **www.BrianMarc.com**

The ME-Story

I have a name for all the commentary in the mind. It's called the ME-Story. The ME-Story is all the thoughts about me. It's the constant narrative in your mind. It's the conversation that you keep going that includes your critique of yourself and others. It's the doubts, the fears, and the worries. It's the way in which you are always trying to figure things out, troubleshooting your life. All of this is the ME-Story.

What you have to realize is that the core of your attention is usually stuck in the ME-Story. You wake up in the ME-Story. You go to bed in the ME-Story. You may even dream in the ME-Story. You think about what you are going to do, what you did, your relationships, and so forth. Your mind just keeps going, bombarding you with thoughts about everything from getting toilet paper, to calling somebody, how we're feeling, if we're okay, if we're not okay, if we're going to get what we want, if we're not going to get what we want. Your attention remains focused on all these thoughts - the ME-Story. On and on it goes.

Everything revolves around you in the ME-Story. And it is very seductive. It becomes your only perspective. You're the lead in your own private movie. When you sleep, your movie shuts down for a moment, but the minute you open your eyes, the whole movie begins again. If you tell the truth...it's exhausting!

Image what it would be like to get a break from the ME-Story. What would that be like? A retreat from the mind. I can tell you right now, it's profoundly wonderful. It's quite a relief to be released from the mind - to be released from the barrage of thoughts, from the survival mind that's constantly trying to defend itself, to know itself, to figure things out, and to be okay.

What Is Your Mind And How Does It Keep Your Attention Stuck In It?

As I stated above, all suffering and unhappiness is the result of identification with mind. Suffering is having your attention stuck in your mind. But what is the mind, really? How does the mind manage to keep your attention? I've already described the mind and the ME-Story - the thoughts and narrative about me and everything that happens to me. But why is it that this creates suffering? Afterall, mind, the ME-Story, is little more than some neural pathways and firing synapses.

The reason that being stuck in the mind causes suffering is because the nature of mind is to divide. All thought creates separation. This is why the thought or belief that "all is one" isn't the same as the reality of experiencing "unity" - because thought is about separation, not unity. So when you are stuck in your mind you can only experience separation, which is painful.

Before thought, outside of mind, everything is already deep meditation. When you "get out of your mind", you experience peace, stillness, and Oneness. This is your True-OneSelf. Everyone has had experiences of this. But then, when you get stuck back in your mind, you believe yourself to be separate again.

I say that everyone has had the experience of Oneness, but sometimes people don't believe that. So I will give you a few examples to show you that you have had this experience.

For a moment, think of a time when you've been in nature

and you became awestruck. Remember a specific time in your life in nature where you looked out at some great vista, a sunrise, a sunset, a canyon, a mountain, and for a moment you were just like "wow!" There was just awe. Afterwards your mind might say, "this is beautiful." Mind likes to label your experience like that. But before that labeling, in that moment of awe, there was stillness. There was connection. You were there, and you were NOT there. There was Oneness. You were out of your mind.

Orgasm is another common experience that is out of mind. If you look at the moment of the peak of sexual orgasm, you'll notice that you experience the "now" - the quieting of mind. During orgasm you experience an explosion that is completely inclusive and completely free of mind.

So, you see that we've all had that experience of Oneness. And, in fact, that experience of your True-OneSelf is actually available right here, right now, all the time. It's not that nature or orgasm created Oneness. Oneness is always here. It's just that in nature or during orgasm, for a moment, you're taken out of your mind. Out of mind you experience the unchanged ground state.

So hopefully now you can see that Oneness, your True-OneSelf, is always present, but being stuck in your mind obscures it. You can see that getting out of your mind is immensely pleasurable and desirable. But what created the mind in the first place?

So how does the ME-Story get built? To begin with, the ME-Story is built into your DNA. You are programmed to survive as an individual. Your DNA creates the ME-Story so that you will have drive and ambition and so that you will protect yourself. Next, the story of me gets reinforced by society. You are given a name. You are encouraged to plan for your future. Society gives you beliefs and morals. All of this is useful, of course, but unquestioned, it all adds to your trance. In *Access Points*, we call it the Individual Mind Trance, or IMT. And if you try to rebel against society by rejecting beliefs and morals, then this still just reinforces your trance - now it's the ME-Story as a rebel.

And then eventually, you begin to carve out your own unique journey in life in which you form your own beliefs and your own opinions. You form your own identity and self-image. This is yet another layer in your IMT.

Access Points will help you to see this more clearly in your own life. You will see that your whole identity is a trance formed by thoughts, concepts, labels, beliefs and descriptions. The IMT is basically the collection of all your patterns for survival. And when you are stuck in your mind, you suffer any time that your identity is threatened, which happens all the time. So you suffer all the time. But when you shift your attention out of your mind, you experience peace and freedom.

The Survival Machine - The Operating System Of The Mind

The mind is programmed to survive. That is its function. It is what I call a *survival machine*. The mind's main goal is to protect itself and ensure its preservation. It's always on alert, on the lookout for danger. This is the operating system of the mind. Picture it like a little Apple computer we put on your mind. This operating system has many functionalities to enlist you in its efforts to survive by trying to convince you that you *are* the mind. Your Identity is maintained as the mind. It entrances you with the ME-Story, so when the mind is threatened, you mistakenly also believe that you are threatened as well.

The mind has tremendous power. Much of human experience comes through the mind. But the power of the mind pales in comparison with the power and vastness of infinite intelligence. Infinite intelligence is the ground of being. What we're all really looking for is this place of rest, this place of knowing ourselves deeply. This place of peace is what true meditation brings and teaches us. And that is beyond the mind, greater than the mind. But this vastness and infinite power feels threatening to the mind, and so the mind works harder to keep you entranced.

The operating system of the mind uses two primary strategies to keep you entranced and captivated. The first is fear, to protect the body. The second is building a special identity, a some-"body", a separate individual who must be maintained and defended.

Fear Of Being Destroyed

The survival machine's primary feature is to keep you safe and to not be destroyed. It does that with fear - the fear of death. It's in your genes. It's in your reptilian brain to protect yourself and keep yourself from being destroyed, to not allow any harm to come to your physical body.

Imagine that you're in a small tribe of people living hundreds of years ago. You're out in this vast desert. Night falls and it is dark - pitch black. You don't even have fire, and you get lost from the tribe. You're all alone. The unknown is all around you. You start to hear the sounds of animals. Growls. Roars. Perhaps you have a weapon in your hand. But wait, let's up the ante a little. Instead of being alone, let's say you have a loved one with you, a partner, a husband, a wife. If you have a child, better yet. Imagine they're with you. Imagine the animals are walking toward you. You know that if someone gets lost from the tribe, there's a good chance they're not coming back. The mind's job is to find a way to survive and to protect you. Fear is necessary. It's not about getting rid of fear. It's not that fear is wrong. It's a primary function of this operating system.

Here is another story to better help you get a sense of the survival machine and fear. Imagine you're in the water swimming and you see an enormous, hungry-looking shark coming toward you. In this situation, you have to experience fear in order to survive. If you don't experience fear, you're not going to swim away very quickly. It'd probably be smart to get away from a shark when it's coming up on you, but if you felt no sensation of fear - no inclination in your mind/body system for that primal survival instinct - the shark will start eating your foot. You'd be like "Hey shark. How you doing, man?" It starts eating up to your knee. You say, "Oh, cool man, let's hang out." That's silly, of course, but you get the idea. The survival machine uses fear to keep the physical body safe.

We now live in a society where a lot of us are lucky not to have to worry about physical harm coming to us most of time. Many of us living in today's modern world know that being physically destroyed at any moment is not our biggest concern. But the mind continues this survival programming anyway, and so we become afraid of all sorts of things made-up by the mind. But ultimately, the mind uses fear to keep your attention. Because if you don't identify with the mind, then it has no identity - it is no one. The mind fears being destroyed if it doesn't have your attention.

Being Somebody Special - Identity

As we just learned, the number one function of the operating system of the survival animal is to protect its *physical* body. Yet, what most people don't realize is, as much as the ego mind is trying to keep its body safe from physical destruction, it's also trying to protect its *identity* as a somebody - a separate individual. Special. Different. Unique. This is really crucial to comprehend. In fact, this understanding itself can change everything for you if you really take it in deeply.

I'm not putting down your uniqueness. You are undeniably unique. You have a unique DNA unlike any other human being in the world. You have unique gifts to share. I'm talking about the structure and the function of the ego mind that's programmed to survive. It must protect its separate body *and* its separate identity. You see, that's the whole crux of suffering. Kind of why Buddha said life is suffering, because the ego structure, in trying to maintain physical survival, is also trying to make sure that it's not going to have its separate sense of identity destroyed; it has to substantiate and prove that it's somebody separate and special. In maintaining itself as separate, it also maintains suffering because if you are a separate individual, then you can be destroyed.

So it is constantly protecting your identification with your mind - the "ME".

Your mind can think you're the worst "ME", most unworthy person there is - that you're so low, you're no good. But then the mind has to be the *best* of the no good. It has to say "there's nobody worse than me." The deflated ego. Or the mind believes it's the best, the greatest, a winner, it's so awesome. The inflated ego. It believes either extreme about itself, or anywhere in between. All defensiveness of our personalities comes from this. The point is that the mind is always working to build up and maintain a sense that you are something special that it must protect. So if you believe that you are the best, and something happens that contradicts that idea of yourself, then you have to defend your idea of self. Or if you believe you are the worst, and then something contradicts that, then you also defend the idea of self.

As long the mind can convince you that it is someone - the worst or the best someone - then it's succeeding in entrancing you. The mind has to convince you that you're somebody special because if you're not somebody, then you're nobody. That's the last thing the mind wants is to be...no-body.

The special "ME" is the only thing that stands in the way of knowing true happiness. All the doubts, fears, worries, figuring things out, and stress come from your identification with your mind.

Main Programs Of The Survival Machine

A crucial way to *Access* your True-OneSelf, and "get out of your mind" to experience the peace of meditation and Oneness, is to become aware of the mind's programs as they are operating.

In this section you will realize the mind's patterns it uses to maintain the separate identity of the survival machine. As you consciously see these patterns operating, you are shifting from being stuck in the mind pattern to being a witness of the pattern. <u>The more you are the witness of patterns, the more you are shifting to freedom.</u> This is simple and profound, and it can change your way of life. Shifting your attention "out of your mind" to the witness, or awareness, of the patterns, leads to an experience of freedom and the meditative state. So what are the main programs of the mind? By realizing these main programs, you will start to see through the mind's deceptions.

Before we move forward, imagine that the mind has you on a leash, like a dog being led on a walk. This is the reality for most people. Most people live their whole lives being kept on a leash by the mind. The mind's programs and patterns are in control of your consciousness. But now imagine how wonderful it would be to reverse that so that you are no longer on a leash. Instead, *you can lead the mind* on a leash. As you practice Access Points, and SSBB, this is exactly what will happen.

Avoid The Unknown

The main job of the mind is to avoid the unknown and keep itself safe. Ironically, it is when we we learn to take risks that we actually propel ourselves in life. It's all because we've let go of the known and jumped into the unknown. They say that takes heart. Yet, the mind cannot exist in the unknown, so it fervently holds on to the known with all its might. The mind uses the main programs of the mind to cling to thoughts by labeling, creating problems, figuring things out, and pretending to know everything in order to avoid the unknown. There is fear in the unknown. There is no security in the unknown. The future is the unknown, and the survival mind sees the unknown as death. Since we really do not know for sure what will happen in the future, in truth, you could die at any moment. This creates anxiety for the mind, so it avoids this truth with memories of the past or imagination of the future. It does all it can to keep attention with thoughts and maintain Identity with the mind. Of course, the truth is we are always in the unknown. The is unknown is actually the mystery and vibrancy of life. An even deeper truth is that in the unknown is a portal to your True-OneSelf, which is the source of creativity and excitement.

It is when we dive directly into the unknown and experience the discomfort of ego/mind that we can find profound presence and peace. When you learn to be comfortable with the unknown by being present, the mind can't run you. Now you hold the leash.

Create A Problem To Solve It

One main function of the operating system is to create a problem to solve it. The mind is always doing one or the other - creating a problem or solving a problem. The mind is a problem-making machine. This is one of the mind's strategies for remaining in control and keeping you on a leash. It leads you around by constantly creating problems which it then sets out to solve. Having problems to solve is one way in which the mind keeps you identified with the it - as the problem solver. It is constantly trying to figure things out to avoid the unknown. It keeps the drama of the ME-Story alive, and focuses on thoughts, problems, and having to solve them. This creates a vast amount of struggle and suffering in life and takes much of our energy. So you set out to find a solution to the problems created by the mind. But as soon as you find a solution, your mind creates another problem. It is when we become aware of this cycle and learn how to shift out of the mind's problem/solution pattern, becoming the witness of the pattern, that you can access your True-OneSelf. In doing this, you will experience a great renewal of energy as most of the things we thought were "problems" in life become not as big a deal as we once thought.

So what do you do about this vicious cycle? Simply begin to recognize the pattern is occurring. Your mind is trying to entrance you with the problems that it creates and all its thinking to figure out a solution. It is *key* to not try to stop the pattern. It is a fundamental program of the mind, and it is futile to battle it. Simply notice the pattern is operating. Don't take my word for it. For this to really help you "get out of your mind", you need to take these moments to be aware. Check throughout your day and see if your mind is creating a problem or solving one. Become aware of the pattern.

The more you are the witness of patterns, the more you are shifting to freedom.

Label, Dissect, Compartmentalize

So we've seen the mind creating a problem to solve it. It's trying to figure things out because the more that it knows, the further it is from the unknown, the safer it is. It's surviving.

Now let's take a look at another of the main features of this operating system that keeps us identified with our mind and in survival mode: The mind's protecting itself by always labeling, dissecting, and compartmentalizing things. It's constantly doing this. It's labelling in order to separate. It dissects to further label in smaller details to substantiate that it knows and understands things. It then ultimately compartmentalizes the pieces and puts them in the right spot so it feels safe thinking it knows where everything is, to be referenced in the future. So it's all a game of survival, safety, and upholding the "somebody special" individual identity.

The mind constantly labels and dissects things based on the past. Once it's seen something, the mind believes that it knows what that thing is - compartmentalizing. The mind feels that it has to label everything. The mind exists in separation, therefore, it labels everything around you to keep everything separate from you. In this way, it can maintain your sense of yourself as an individual and avoid the deeper reality of Oneness.

So notice that because the mind is always labeling and dissecting everything, it never has a direct experience of anything. It separates everything. Photons hit your eyeballs, sending electrical signals to your brain, and suddenly your mind tells you that there is an apple over there. But it's just giving you a label. The label isn't the direct experience. The label is creating separation of you over here and apple over there. But what is the actual direct experience? *You* can know this, but the *mind* cannot. Let me give you an example.

Imagine that you are going to smell a rose. Now, in the moment that you go to smell a rose, your mind already knows what a rose is. This is because your mind has given it a label. Your mind already knows that it's going to smell a rose. If you have smelled a rose before, then the mind will remember the smell of a rose that you've smelled before - not *this* rose, not *this* present experience, but a memory from the past. It reaches into the compartment and it remembers "*rose*". So the mind is already ready to produce that remembered response.

What can you notice from this example? When the mind gives you a label, you may accept that label and essentially live in the mind instead of directly experiencing what is happening right now. The mind's constant labeling and dissecting of things brings us one step away from the real moment. This present moment that is now, we never get to experience this reality because we're always in our heads, one step away from it. Either going into the future, or into the past, the mind is never present or in the moment.

The same thing that happens with the rose happens with all experiences. The mind even labels emotions - anger, fear, unworthiness - so that you live in the mind's thoughts *about* these emotions instead of *having* the direct experience. Your mind has fearful thoughts about these emotions, and so you live your whole life running as far away from them as you can.

But remember, it's all in your mind. It's not the direct

experience. In smelling the rose, the mind already has a label and the understanding of how it's going to smell. But on the other hand, you have a choice to truly be present to the direct experience of the smell. Then you and rose become the direct experience of Oneness. The same is true of emotion - directly experience an emotion, and you and emotion are unified as OneSelf.

Between you and rose, or you and emotion, there's nothing really keeping you separate. But the mind is so fast and quick with its labels and its ideas. It already knows the smell or the feeling. And it already has a judgment of good or bad. By dissecting every single thing and every moment, the mind separates everything, and we miss out on "smelling the roses." We miss out on the direct experience of life - of Oneness, of our True-OneSelf. We miss out on the direct experience of truly meeting other people and life's moments. We miss out by being so caught up in the labeling program of the mind that the direct experience of life, where richness, vastness, and beauty come from, is lost.

So, again, like with Create a Problem/Solve it, simply begin to recognize the pattern is occurring. Your mind is trying to entrance you by labeling, dissecting and compartment-talizing. Do not try to stop the pattern. Simply notice the pattern is operating. Check throughout your days and see when your mind is labeling, dissecting, or referencing a compartment. Become aware of the pattern.

Remember, all of these mind programs are running on auto-pilot, like a robot. They keep you actively "stuck" in your mind. The more and more we simply recognize these patterns, the more you will know peace and then can shift further by using *SSBB*.

Get Out Of Your Mind, Not Rid Of The Mind - The Witness

By now you are probably starting to see just how much trouble the mind seems to create. It labels, separates, judges, fears, and creates all your suffering. So what should you do to improve your situation? Getting rid of your mind and thoughts would seem like the easiest solution, right? Well, this is the way in which many people have misunderstood spiritual and enlightenment teachings for thousands of years.

See, the idea that you're going to get rid of your mind/ego is crazy. That is just the mind beating up and judging the mind. It is only the mind/ego that can tell the mind to get rid of itself. You see, all this occurs in thoughts and in the separation of mind. This is still taking place in the ME-Story. True freedom is *outside* of the mind. Trying to destroy the ego or destroy the mind is just more suffering.

True freedom is about connecting with your True-OneSelf - identifying with your True-OneSelf rather than your mind. You don't have to get rid of your mind. You don't have to fix your mind. The mind's function is its function. Remember how I told you earlier that the mind is holding you on a leash? That's because you're stuck *in your mind*. Get out of your mind, and then you hold the mind on a leash. Then it's no longer the problem. As we said earlier, meditation really is shifting your attention "out of your mind", and the way to start doing that is to watch or witness it. You shift attention to the witness, or "witness consciousness". It is easier than you would think to recognize the witness. Imagine there is a camera in the room, away from you, looking at you - it sees you there reading this book. Can you be aware of that perspective now? Check this out. You are aware of seeing these words in this book. You are aware of standing or sitting right now. Now be aware of that camera's perspective, the witness perspective, that sees you from "over there" reading the book.

You probably realized it was easy to notice that perspective. Why is it easy? Because awareness is not located in your body or through your eyes. Awareness is always here and ever present - you will discover awareness is your True-OneSelf. This exercise shows you the space which attention can shift to..."out of the mind". Although it may be easy to recognize this witness perspective in a moment, it might seem difficult to keep attention out of the mind and on this awareness itself. That's where *Stop Smile Breathe Be*, or any of the *Access Points*, comes in. Just doing *SSBB* shifts you out of your mind to awareness, Oneness, your True-OneSelf.

So how do you start to apply this in your life? Awareness is the key to true freedom. Awareness is true power. Awareness of the mind is freedom of the mind. When you start becoming aware of the mind looking to protect itself, then you are starting to step out of the mind. Then the mind doesn't have you on a leash any longer. Simply continue to *notice all the programs that the mind operates*. The computer on your mind is just running the programs of the operating system. Watch how it tries to entrance you and prevent you from having a direct experience of the moment.

Soon, as you are watching or witnessing the mind, you will be able to use the mind's programs as a trigger. The moment you are aware of the labels, fear, stress, or problem/solution that your mind is running, you will be able to shift your attention and connect with stillness and peace. So what was once unconsciously creating your suffering can now become the key to your awakening to true inner and outer peace. Soon, when you notice any of these patterns, they will be triggers for you to *Stop Smile Breathe Be*. In the full 6-week course, **Access Points - The Modern Life Meditation Plan**, we practice witnessing these patterns and utilizing *Access Points* on a daily basis. Participants begin to live life "out of their mind" and experience the peace of meditation throughout the day. This is also possible for you now as you begin to witness the mind's programs and apply *SSBB*.

The Choice - Survive Or Thrive

Now I want you to see that you have a choice. Either you can survive or you can thrive. Survival is about being caught up in the ME-Story - a life of stress, fear, defensiveness, anxiety and unhappiness. Survival means being caught up in the mind, caught up in trying to protect your image of yourself as somebody special.

On the other hand, thriving is all about living a life of clarity, creativity, and ecstatic enjoyment. When you shift away from survival and let go of the ME-Story, you also let go of stress, anxiety, worry, and fear. Thriving is recognizing and connecting with your True-OneSelf. When you are thriving you are able to meet life, be present to emotion, be present to all your relationships, and enjoy it all. Thriving is about being free - having a moment-to-moment freedom.

The choice is as simple as where you place your attention. If you place your attention on the mind then you are choosing suffering - choosing to survive. In survival, there's no place for rest. There's no space for rest when your mind is preoccupied with survival.

On the other hand, to thrive is to come from a place of True-OneSelf, to come from a place of clarity, to come from a place of peace. Soon I will teach you one of the *Access Points* that will allow you to begin to thrive. As you practice *SSBB* on a daily basis for 1 to 3 minutes at a time, you will begin to shift to recognizing your vast True-OneSelf, and you will know that peace is available to you moment-to-moment, always. By choosing to thrive, you are choosing to live from your greatest source, from your Divine birthright of knowing the truth of who you are. From there comes the greatest expression of yourself. As you continue to choose to thrive, you recognize that your True-OneSelf is the source of true power and the source of you living your truest purpose. It is from here that your greatest talents can be shared.

The Wisdom Of Discernment

In life, most everything changes - things come and go. But there is that which is unchanging - the ground of being, your True-OneSelf. That which is unchanging is the background on which all that changes occurs. Mind is changing while your True-OneSelf is unchanging. True freedom, true meditation, is taking your attention off of what changes and turning it to what is unchanging. You can rest fully in that which is always here. And in order to do this, it is necessary to learn how to discern between what changes and what is unchanging.

Discernment is learning how to tell the difference between what comes and goes and that which is always here. What comes and goes is unreliable. But the unchanging stillness of your True-OneSelf is completely trustworthy because it is always here for you. You have given your allegiance to your mind, and, therefore, you have been let down because the mind is not trustworthy. So now you must learn to tell the difference between the mind and that which is reliable and always here.

When you start to discern the difference between which is which, you also start recognizing that you're caught up in your mind most of the time. You know this because you see that your attention is caught up in things that change. When your attention is in your mind then you are restless, anxious, and unfulfilled. Yet when your attention shifts to that which is infinite, then you are instantly fulfilled. There's fulfillment there because it's already full. That's where rest, peace and freedom come from.

All emotions come and go. All thoughts come and go. All sensations in the body come and go. Take a look and see this for yourself. You can do this by repeating an exercise that you did previously: Moving Attention. Look at your shirt and just notice what color it is. You need no effort to move your attention to notice something. Soon I will teach you a specific way that you can use this same "Power of Attention" in order to shift your core attention to Being. But before I get to that, I'd like to share with you an exercise that you can use to learn to easily discern between that which comes and goes and that which is unchanging.

Exercise: Past To Now Moment - Being Always Here

I want you to remember a time when you were in high school. Take a moment, close your eyes if you need to, and just remember a time when you were in high school. Use the first memory that comes to mind.

Now, in your imagination, go back to that time and picture what was happening then. Picture what you were wearing, what you looked like, what was happening around you. Picture it vividly in full-color. What was the first thing you heard, saw, or felt there? Then take a look at what was the next thing you heard, saw, or felt. I want you to go back and just put yourself there. Put yourself in the movie as if you are there now.

How does your hair look? Your clothes? Your face? Your skin? Did you look the same then as you do now? Exactly the same? You look different there than you look right now, correct? So the way you look has changed.

Do you have the same thoughts in that moment as you have now? Or even the same beliefs? The thoughts change...they come and they go. Even if you say you have similar thoughts or way of thinking, no one thought remained all these years. Thoughts come and go.

How did you feel then? Do you have the same exact emotion then as you do now? Usually not. You have matured. Maybe similar emotions occur, but has the same exact emotion remained all these years? Have you felt one emotion constantly, every moment, for years? Of course not, emotions come and go.

Your thoughts have come and gone. Your belief system has changed. Your feelings have changed. How you look has changed. Most everything has changed. Even the atoms and molecules have changed.

Now, notice that right now, you're here. When you came to pick up this book today, or started reading this book, you were here. I'm not talking about some extraordinary experience of "here", as in feeling like the gates of heaven open and you're enlightened. I'm just talking about the simple sense that you *are*. You *are* here. You exist. You may be feeling good or bad, thinking various thoughts, but apart from that, you *are* here. The simple sense that you *are*. You are BEING.

Now, once again, imagine that moment in high school and put yourself there. Are you there? Be in the movie. Check out if you *are*. Do you exist? I'm not asking if you intellectually *know* that you are. Just in that moment in high school - seeing what you're seeing, feeling what you're feeling, are you there? Do you exist? Is that simple sense that you are present? Just the simple sense that you are. You *are* there. Being. Has that changed? Or is it the same as you, here, right now? Being.

And now, I want you to imagine that you are going back to a time when you were even younger, such as when you were in elementary school. Remember a time when you were that young? Go back to that moment, into the movie, full-color. Close your eyes if you need to, and picture that time in elementary school.

What was the first thing you heard, saw, or felt there? Then take a look at what was the next thing you heard, saw, or felt. Notice where you were, what you were wearing, what you heard, and what you were feeling. I want you to go back and just put yourself there. Put yourself in the movie as if you are there now.

Notice the way you look. Do you look the same then as how you looked in high school? Do you look the same as you do now? No, how you look has changed.

Is what you believe to be true about life and yourself, your belief systems, has that changed? Do you have the same thoughts in that moment as you have now? The exact same thoughts you had back in high school? You see, even if a lot of them are similar thoughts throughout your life, your thoughts come and go.

How about your feelings? Do you have the same exact emotions in that moment as you did in back high school? Or the same exact emotions that you have now? Again, maybe similar emotions occur, but has the same exact emotion remained all these years? Have you felt one emotion constantly, every moment, for years? No. Emotions/feelings come and go.

Now, imagine again that moment in elementary school and put yourself there. Be in the movie. Check out if you *are*. Notice that the simple sense that you *are* - Being - is still there. No matter what you were thinking or feeling or seeing, you were *there*. Your sense that you *are*, just that you *are*, that sense is there. And now once again, go to the high school moment/movie. Notice that you *are*. Wherever you are right now reading this book, regardless of what you're thinking, whatever you're doing right now, regardless of how you're feeling or even how you look - are you here? Being? Has the sense that you *are* - Being - ever changed? Take a few moments and explore this. See what comes and goes and what is always here.

Now you can start to have greater discernment. Now you can notice when your attention is all caught up on things that come and go. Things that come and go are not lasting, which means they can't offer true fulfillment or real peace because the struggle, the worry, and the fear are all generated from the coming and going - the temporal. What is solid is that which never comes and goes, and it's actually always been here.

That solid space is Being - simply Being - that is always present.

Now you have experienced Being. For some of you, in the past have fallen deep into Being. You've experienced it in meditation before. Or, like I've said, you've experienced it in nature or during orgasm, whether you think you have or not. So one way or another you have experienced Being, stillness and peace, but you haven't had it stick. Now it's time for it to stick.

If you'd like to go deeper and have me personally guide you through this exercise, register now for *SSBB - Awakening to Your True-OneSelf* - a FREE Live Global online seminar. Sign up at **www.BrianMarc.com**.

The Rain Dance Of Emotions

You've probably had the experience of seeing a storm brewing far away in the sky. We know there's a probable chance of rain. In many ways, this is just like when you start to get frustrated or angry, bothered, stressed, or sad. You start seeing this sadness growing, or this fear growing, or this anger growing. You can see where it's headed, just like you see the storm coming.

When the mind storms happen, you have choices. The first choice is to indulge that anger, that fear or that sadness, and react from it. If it's anger, you can act out, yell, get pissed off, feel frustrated, and have angst in your body. This, of course, causes discomfort and stress to you and to others. You can get sad and depressed. You can indulge the sadness and depression and have a self-pity party. You can feel horrible about yourself. These are some of the ways in which you can indulge the mind storm.

The second choice is to repress. You can repress the sadness, repress the anger, repress the fear. You know what that experience is like too. You feel tension in your body. You get stressed out. You turn into a ticking timebomb. You get an ulcer. So the second choice isn't any better than the first.

Then there's the third choice, and this third choice is what I am offering to you in this book. Instead of indulging or repressing, you have the choice to simply be still. You can shift your attention from your mind to stillness that is already present. You can simply allow the storm to pass.

You know, a long time ago, when people would see a storm

73

coming they would think that G-d was mad at them. Of course, you and I know that is ridiculous, but that is what they believed. They believed that they could appease G-d by doing a certain dance. They would do this dance, this whole charade and this whole dance, and soon enough the clouds would part and the storm would go. So they believed that the dance had worked. But then every time a storm would come they had to do a specific dance because G-d was mad. They had to do this dance so the storm would go away. One day, a tribesman was away from the village. As a storm came in, he didn't do the dance. He just watched, and he noticed, "Oh, the storm still leaves. It comes and it goes no matter what."

Like the storms, all the emotions in your life - anger, fear, unworthiness - will come and they will go. The dramatic dance we all do to deal with these emotions isn't necessary. As King Solomon said, "This too shall pass." *You* can be the person who is able to be still and just witness the emotions and sensations. You do not have to get caught up in the dance to "solve a problem". Instead, you notice that every mental storm comes and goes. You shift out of your mind and experience what doesn't come and go: the peace of Oneness that is always present.

Stop Smile Breathe Be

Now that you've had a chance to explore the Power of Attention and how to discern between what changes and what is unchanging, I'm excited to share with you Stop Smile Breathe Be, or SSBB. I created this Access Point to shift you out of your mind and to your True-OneSelf at any moment. As you begin to do this daily, your suffering begins to fall away. It becomes like a boat caught in a whirlpool - the water will pull it to the center. So, too, will you be pulled to the center of your True-OneSelf.

In just minutes, you will be able to connect to the same profound stillness and peace that all awakened beings know to be their True-OneSelf. You can do this anytime and anywhere. You don't have to plug in your headphones and listen to a meditation track for 30 minutes. You don't have to find a quiet space away from the extreme and busy activity of life. You don't have to close your eyes, sit still, or visualize anything. With SSBB you will receive all the benefits of meditation and live free from struggle and suffering.

SSBB is so easy and the results are so pleasurable that you'll find it convenient to do frequently. So you can easily do SSBB at any time. I want you to commit to doing SSBB at least three times every day. More than that, you should start to use your growing discernment to notice whenever the mind is using any of the main survival programs to create a sense of separation and do SSBB right then! When you notice that the mind is creating fear from the unknown, creating/solving problems, labeling, dissecting, or compartmentalizing, then you will do SSBB. The more you

75

do this, the more you naturally move your attention to your True-OneSelf. Now I'm going to share with you how to do SSBB.

Stop Smile Breathe Be pretty much sums up the four basic steps of SSBB. The first step is STOP. That means that whatever you're doing, you're going to hit the pause button. Pause all that you are doing for a moment. This doesn't mean you can't keep moving, walking or driving. For example, if you're driving in the car, you don't need to pull over. Just STOP (pause), then SMILE. If you're singing along to a song on the radio, you don't need to turn the radio off. Just STOP singing (pause) and SMILE. If you're in the middle of a speech or a conversation, you don't have to "tune out" anyone or anything. Just STOP for a moment (pause) and SMILE. Remember that a single SSBB doesn't require much time, about 30 seconds to 1 minute. So you can be in the grocery check-out line, getting your money out, and still STOP (pause), money in hand - and SMILE. Even the longer forms like the "SSBBx3" require no more than 2 minutes! So step 1, just for a moment, hit the pause button and STOP.

The second step is SMILE. Just as you might guess, this means to put a SMILE on your face. Allow your attention to move and stay on your SMILE. And make it a big SMILE, with teeth showing and all! Don't worry if your SMILE seems forced or unnatural. You don't even have to *feel* like smiling. Just SMILE. The act of smiling, even if you don't feel like it, is very beneficial. This physical act produces lots of positive changes in your physical and mental physiology. In fact, chemically, the mind can't tell the difference between a fake smile or a real smile! So this is really an important step. SMILE and keep your full attention remaining on your SMILE.

The third step is to BREATHE. Of course, this is naturally happening already. However, you now turn your full attention to your BREATH. And with your attention on your BREATH, draw in a deep, long, and steady BREATH through your nose. As you do this, allow your attention to really follow the BREATH inward - you can focus on the sensation of it passing through your nostrils. Feel it as you pull your BREATH in. Continue to follow your BREATH with your attention as it moves deeply through your chest and as you exhale out through your mouth, jaw loose and mouth relaxed. On the exhale, your attention stays with the BREATH and the sensation of it passing over your lips. BREATHE and keep your full attention focused on the inhale and exhale of your BREATH.

And then the fourth step is to BE. You don't have to *do* BEING. A clear sense of BEING will naturally arrive after the breath. For a few moments...simply BE. (Recall the discernment exercise we just did where you realized what doesn't come and go - BEING...the simple sense that you *are*.) You *are* here. You *are* present. You *are* BEING. So in this step, rest in simply BEING. Give your attention fully to this experience of BEING. Receive BEING. Keep attention resting with simply BEING for at least ten seconds, and for those few moments...simply BE. In this, you will have access to the meditative moment - Oneness - your True-OneSelf.

So there you have it. You can do SSBB for no reason at all or when you're stressed out or upset. When you notice your attention is stuck in your thoughts/mind/the ME-Story, or when you recognize the survival machine programs are operating...STOP. Take that pause. Next you SMILE, and as you do this move **all attention** to your SMILE. Even if you don't feel like smiling, just put on a big SMILE anyways. Then you turn your **full attention** to your BREATH. Remember to BREATHE in through your nose and out through your mouth. As you do this, follow your BREATH with your **full attention** on the deep inhale (feel the breath passing through your nostrils) and exhale (feel your breath pass by your lips), and then finally rest in **BEING.** Rest your **full attention** with BEING, on your True-OneSelf, and remain here, SIMPLY BEING, for at least ten seconds or longer. Do this 3 times in a row.

When you start doing SSBB, for *best* results do SSBB three times in a row, called SSBBx3. Try it now:

1. STOP - pause everything. Then instantly...
2. SMILE - Really SMILE. A big SMILE. Put your full attention on that beautiful SMILE.
3. BREATHE - Put your full attention on following the breath in, then EXHALE.
4. BE - Stay there for 10 sec.
5. Repeat SSBB 2 more times.

Throughout the practice of SSBB, don't worry if there's distraction or your mind wanders. That's okay. It doesn't matter. Your mind can think what it wants to think. Remember, you're not trying to get rid of thoughts here. You're just shifting your attention to your Smile, to Breath, and to Being.

Now, of course, SSBB is very simple. So go ahead and do SSBBx3 again right now. Practice it a few times, and notice how easy it is to connect with your True-OneSelf. As you notice how profound it is to connect to true power and true peace you will be inspired to SSBB throughout the day.

If you'd like to go deeper and have me personally guide you in doing SSBB, you can register for my FREE Live Global online seminar: *SSBB - Awakening to Your True-OneSelf.*

Getting The Most Benefits From SSBB

SSBB is a profound and powerful Access Point, and I know that you have already had a taste of that. Now I want to share with you some tips for how you can quickly get the most benefits from SSBB.

First and foremost, you actually have to "do" SSBB to get the benefits. It is so quick and easy that you'll have no problem doing SSBB all the time. At a minimum, make sure you commit to doing SSBB at least three times every day. Set times in your daily calendar or alarms to remind you to SSBB throughout the day. Commit to this, and after just one week you will be amazed at the dramatic results in your life.

Never do SSBB with the intention of getting rid of, or changing, your thoughts or emotions. Instead, have your intention be to shift "out of your mind" and connect to your True-OneSelf. So any time that you notice a thought or feeling that you want to get rid of, let that be a reminder to practice SSBB. Let go of the "get rid of" battle, and release all as you step into SSBB. When you practice SSBB you are just shifting your attention. That is all. You are not getting rid of thoughts or feelings. You are doing SSBB to renew yourself in Oneness.

In order to gain the most benefit from the Smile, hold the Smile throughout. You Stop and Smile. Then hold the Smile as you Breathe, and continue to Smile as you put your attention on Being. Holding the smile like this, even if at first it is a "fake" smile, will *greatly* increase the effects.

For the first 6 weeks, I suggest you re-read the "Main Programs" section in this book once a week. Take time daily to focus on each of the Main Programs: Avoid the Unknown, Create a Problem to Solve It, Label/Dissect/Compartmentalize. At first, focus on a specific program each day. This will help you master noticing all the programs as they operate in your life. The point is, as you sharpen your ability to notice these patterns in operation, you will

1. Shift more and more out of survival/suffering and the IMT (Individual Mind Trance), thus, you will notice the beauty and equanimity of the witness perspective as you connect to the peace of BEING.

2. Learn to do SSBB whenever one of these programs is operating. Over time, they will be triggers to SBBB and ACCESS your True-OneSelf. Again, you're not doing it to get rid of the program (the function of the mind is its function), but to release and shift "out of your mind".

You can do a single SSBB at any time and experience profound stillness and peace. I highly recommend, especially in your first weeks of practice, to do SSBB three times in a row - SSBBx3 - whenever you can. It will help the shift out of your mind, and you will be amazed at how quickly you can go deeply into meditative stillness and freedom no matter what is going on in your life. Once you've got SSBBx3 down and you experience the shift to Being and peace regularly, then a single SSBB will produce the same results.

The more you do SSBB, and the more you commit to connecting with your True-OneSelf, the more profound your changes will be. There's no doubt that creating a new habit takes a bit of work, and this is the most wonderful habit you could ever create! This is the habit of turning away from the stress of mind and to the peace of being that is your True-OneSelf.

Experiencing the peace of meditation in any moment is now available to you. You can live an Awake Life. Not once in awhile or when you only have a peak blissful or happy experience, but daily. No matter what is occurring in life, good or bad, happy or sad - you can know inner-peace.

Get Started Now

I am so excited that you have begun this journey of connecting with your True-OneSelf, moment-to-moment in your life. You have the tools to thrive, now choose to do so. You can do this...and you deserve it!!

There's no doubt that creating a new habit takes a bit of work. This is the most wonderful habit you could ever create! This is the habit of turning away from the stress of mind and towards the endless peace of being that is your True-OneSelf. At first you will get hits of meditation a few times a day, then more and more you will notice meditation moment-to-moment.

Right now I invite you to say "yes" to your True-OneSelf, and commit to doing SSBB at least three times every day.

Put it on your day planner. Set alarms on your phone.

In fact, put down this book and go ahead and do it right now. :)

Set alarms for **three** times tomorrow to do SSBB.

If you do it more often, like every time wake up and go to bed, or you stop at a red light when driving, even better. Commit to doing SSBB any time you notice that you are stuck in your mind. It only takes a minute. Give yourself this amazing gift!

Do This Next

I have a gift for you that will greatly support your success: *SSBB - Awakening to Your True-OneSelf* - a FREE Live Global online seminar where I personally teach you the Access Points processes and guides you through all of the exercises in this book, including SSBB. People report lasting transformative shifts in this seminar. Take advantage of this Modern Meditation training. It is upwards of $10,000 to work with me in private, yet I am offering this seminar for FREE because I am committed to your awakening and sharing this message with as many people as possible. We can all help a global *SHIFT* to peace and Oneness.

Go to **www.BrianMarc.com** and register NOW.

If you found this book helpful on your journey to inner-peace and Awakening to Your True-OneSelf, and you would like to learn all 5 of the Access POINTS, you will have the opportunity to enroll in the full 6-week program, learn all the Access Points, and have a daily plan to follow, daily guidance, and meet live twice a week with me, and have the support of a like minded community on the same journey. Sign up at www.BrianMarc.com/pages/events.

There is a movement happening - a movement of awakening to our True-OneSelf that is the ultimate source of joy, creativity, and connection. As you Awaken to your True-OneSelf, I invite you to join me and the others who are dawning on the truth, at the leading edge of consciousness. Let SSBB be your Access Point to this whole new world - a world with the tremendous potential of human evolution. So make this commitment today. Right now. Connect with your True-OneSelf. And open the gateway to a whole new life.

PLEASE WRITE A REVIEW OF THIS BOOK

If you liked this book, it would be fabulous if you would write a review of it on site of the retailer from which you got the book

I know, I know. You think it doesn't matter. And it is sort of obnoxious that I ask you to take a minute from your valuable time to do something like write a review of this book.

But actually, reviews are really, really helpful. And that's the reason I ask.

See, the way the retailers work is they help potential readers to discover new books, *but only if those books have* recent *reviews.*

So if you liked this book and would like others to be able to discover it, please do take a moment right now to write a review and post it on the site of the retailer from which you got this book. It really does make a difference. Thank you.

SSBB Practical Applications Guide

Now that you've learned the how to do of SSBB, I'd like to share a gift with you. It shows you how you can use SSBB for specific purposes such as forgiveness, purpose, creativity, and releasing pain. To download this FREE addendum, Go to

www.BrianMarc.com/p/applications-of-ssbb